EMMANUEL JOSEPH

Sounds of the Ancients, How Rhetoric from Lost Civilizations Can Transform Modern Oratory

Copyright © 2025 by Emmanuel Joseph

All rights reserved. No part of this publication may be reproduced, stored or transmitted in any form or by any means, electronic, mechanical, photocopying, recording, scanning, or otherwise without written permission from the publisher. It is illegal to copy this book, post it to a website, or distribute it by any other means without permission.

First edition

*This book was professionally typeset on Reedsy.
Find out more at reedsy.com*

Contents

1	Chapter 1: The Echoes Begin	1
2	Chapter 2: The Mesopotamian Masters	3
3	Chapter 3: The Egyptian Eloquence	5
4	Chapter 4: The Greek Revolution	7
5	Chapter 5: The Roman Legacy	9
6	Chapter 6: The Silence of the Indus Valley	11
7	Chapter 7: The Mesoamerican Voice	13
8	Chapter 8: The African Echoes	15
9	Chapter 9: The Asian Harmony	17
10	Chapter 10: The Native American Spirit	19
11	Chapter 11: The Renaissance Revival	21
12	Chapter 12: The Modern Symphony	23

1

Chapter 1: The Echoes Begin

The art of speech is as old as humanity itself. Long before microphones and stages, ancient voices carried wisdom across generations, shaping societies and sparking revolutions. These voices, though silent now, still whisper to us through fragments of texts, carvings, and oral traditions. Their rhetoric was not just about persuasion; it was about survival, connection, and the pursuit of truth. In a world where modern communication often feels shallow, the depth of ancient oratory offers a beacon of hope. By revisiting these lost civilizations, we can rediscover the power of words to move, inspire, and transform.

The ancients understood something we often forget: speech is not just a tool but a reflection of the soul. Their words were imbued with purpose, whether to honor the gods, unite a tribe, or challenge injustice. They spoke not only to the mind but to the heart, weaving logic and emotion into a seamless tapestry. Today, as we navigate a sea of information overload, their approach reminds us to speak with intention. The echoes of their wisdom call us to slow down, to choose our words carefully, and to remember that every speech is an opportunity to leave a lasting impact.

What made ancient rhetoric so enduring was its adaptability. From the deserts of Egypt to the mountains of Peru, each civilization developed its own unique style of oratory, tailored to its culture and needs. Yet, beneath the surface differences, there were universal principles: clarity, authenticity, and respect for the audience. These principles transcend time and place, offering a foundation for modern speakers to build upon. By studying the ancients, we can learn to adapt our own communication to the needs of our listeners, creating a bridge between past and present.

The journey into ancient rhetoric is not just an academic exercise; it is a personal one. As we explore the speeches of kings, philosophers, and storytellers, we begin to see ourselves in their words. Their struggles, triumphs, and aspirations mirror our own, reminding us of the shared human experience. This connection is the essence of great oratory: the ability to speak not just to a crowd but to the individual soul. In embracing the wisdom of the ancients, we can find our own voice and use it to uplift others.

The sounds of the ancients are not lost; they are waiting to be heard. By listening to their echoes, we can transform modern oratory into a force for good. This book is an invitation to embark on that journey, to explore the rich tapestry of ancient rhetoric, and to bring its timeless lessons into our lives. Let us begin with an open mind and a willing heart, ready to learn from those who came before us.

2

Chapter 2: The Mesopotamian Masters

In the fertile crescent of Mesopotamia, the world's first great civilizations emerged, and with them, the earliest forms of structured oratory. The Sumerians and Akkadians used speech to govern, worship, and record history. Their rhetoric was both practical and poetic, blending the mundane with the divine. Kings delivered proclamations to assert their authority, while priests chanted prayers to invoke the gods. These early speakers understood that words had the power to shape reality, a belief that still resonates today.

One of the most striking features of Mesopotamian rhetoric was its use of repetition and rhythm. Speeches were often structured like hymns, with recurring phrases that reinforced key ideas. This technique not only made the words memorable but also created a sense of unity among listeners. Modern speakers can learn from this approach, using rhythm and repetition to emphasize their message and connect with their audience on a deeper level. The ancients knew that the way something is said is just as important as what is said.

Another hallmark of Mesopotamian oratory was its reliance on storytelling. Myths and legends were not just entertainment; they were tools for teaching moral lessons and preserving cultural values. The Epic of Gilgamesh, for example, is a masterclass in narrative persuasion, using the hero's journey to explore themes of mortality, friendship, and the search for meaning. By incorporating storytelling into their speeches, modern orators can make their messages more relatable and impactful.

Mesopotamian rhetoric also highlights the importance of context. Speeches were tailored to specific occasions, whether a coronation, a harvest festival, or a military campaign. This attention to context ensured that the message was relevant and timely. In today's fast-paced world, where audiences are constantly bombarded with information, this lesson is more important than ever. By understanding the context in which we speak, we can craft messages that resonate with our listeners and address their needs.

Finally, the Mesopotamians remind us that oratory is a communal act. Their speeches were not delivered in isolation but as part of a larger dialogue between speaker and audience. This sense of connection is something modern speakers often overlook. By fostering a sense of community through our words, we can create a space where ideas can flourish and change can begin. The Mesopotamian masters may be long gone, but their legacy lives on in the power of speech.

3

Chapter 3: The Egyptian Eloquence

In the land of the Nile, speech was considered a divine gift, a bridge between the mortal and the eternal. The ancient Egyptians believed that words had the power to create and destroy, to heal and to harm. This sacred view of language infused their rhetoric with a sense of reverence and purpose. Pharaohs used speeches to assert their divine right to rule, while scribes recorded their words for posterity. Even in death, the spoken word played a central role, as spells and incantations guided the soul to the afterlife.

One of the key features of Egyptian oratory was its use of symbolism. Hieroglyphs were not just a form of writing but a visual language that conveyed complex ideas through images. This reliance on symbolism extended to their speeches, where metaphors and allegories were used to illustrate abstract concepts. Modern speakers can draw inspiration from this approach, using vivid imagery to make their messages more engaging and memorable. A well-chosen metaphor can illuminate an idea in a way that plain language cannot.

The Egyptians also understood the importance of preparation. Speeches were carefully crafted, with every word chosen for its impact. This meticulous attention to detail reflects a deep respect for the audience and the occasion. In an age of instant communication, where spontaneity is often valued over preparation, this lesson is particularly relevant. By taking the time to refine our words, we can ensure that our message is clear, concise, and compelling.

Another hallmark of Egyptian rhetoric was its emphasis on harmony. Speeches were designed to create a sense of balance and order, reflecting the Egyptian belief in Ma'at, the principle of cosmic harmony. This focus on balance can be seen in the structure of their speeches, which often followed a clear and logical progression. Modern speakers can apply this principle by organizing their thoughts in a way that is easy to follow, creating a sense of coherence and flow.

Finally, the Egyptians remind us that oratory is an act of service. Whether addressing the gods or the people, the speaker's goal was to uplift and inspire. This selfless approach to speech is a powerful reminder that the true purpose of oratory is not to impress but to connect. By speaking with humility and sincerity, we can create a lasting impact that transcends time and space. The eloquence of the Egyptians is a testament to the enduring power of words.

4

Chapter 4: The Greek Revolution

The ancient Greeks are often credited with revolutionizing the art of oratory, turning it into a disciplined and philosophical practice. In the bustling agora of Athens, speech became the lifeblood of democracy. Citizens gathered to debate laws, policies, and ideas, relying on the power of persuasion to shape their city's future. Figures like Socrates, Plato, and Aristotle studied rhetoric not just as a skill but as a moral responsibility. Their insights laid the groundwork for modern public speaking, emphasizing the importance of logic, ethics, and emotional appeal.

One of the most enduring contributions of Greek rhetoric is the concept of the three modes of persuasion: ethos, pathos, and logos. Ethos refers to the speaker's credibility, pathos to the emotional connection with the audience, and logos to the logical structure of the argument. These principles remain the cornerstone of effective communication today. By balancing these elements, modern speakers can craft messages that are both convincing and compelling, appealing to the head and the heart.

The Greeks also understood the importance of audience analysis. A skilled orator, they believed, must know their listeners—their values, fears, and aspirations. This principle is evident in the speeches of Demosthenes, who tailored his messages to resonate with the concerns of his fellow Athenians. In an era of global communication, where audiences are more diverse than ever, this lesson is invaluable. By understanding our listeners, we can speak to their needs and build a genuine connection.

Another hallmark of Greek oratory was its emphasis on practice and discipline. Demosthenes, for instance, was said to have practiced speaking with pebbles in his mouth to improve his diction. This dedication to mastery reminds us that great speaking is not innate but cultivated. Modern speakers can draw inspiration from this commitment to excellence, recognizing that every speech is an opportunity to refine their craft.

Finally, the Greeks remind us that oratory is a tool for justice and truth. In the hands of a skilled speaker, words can challenge tyranny, expose corruption, and inspire change. This noble purpose is perhaps the greatest legacy of Greek rhetoric. By embracing this ideal, modern speakers can use their voices not just to inform or entertain but to make the world a better place. The Greek revolution in oratory is a testament to the transformative power of speech.

5

Chapter 5: The Roman Legacy

The Romans inherited the Greek tradition of oratory and adapted it to suit their own ambitions and values. In the Senate halls and courtrooms of Rome, rhetoric became a weapon of power and persuasion. Figures like Cicero and Quintilian elevated the art of speech to new heights, emphasizing the importance of structure, style, and delivery. Their works remain essential reading for anyone seeking to master the art of persuasion.

One of the key contributions of Roman rhetoric is its focus on practicality. Unlike the Greeks, who often viewed oratory as a philosophical pursuit, the Romans saw it as a tool for achieving concrete results. Cicero's speeches, for example, were designed to win cases, sway public opinion, and defend the Republic. This pragmatic approach is particularly relevant today, where the ability to communicate effectively is often the key to success in business, politics, and beyond.

The Romans also placed a strong emphasis on decorum—the idea that a speaker's style should match the occasion and audience. A funeral oration, for instance, required a different tone than a political debate. This principle of adaptability is crucial in modern communication, where speakers must navigate a wide range of contexts and audiences. By tailoring our style to the situation, we can ensure that our message is received as intended.

Another hallmark of Roman rhetoric was its attention to delivery. The

Romans understood that how a speech is delivered can be just as important as its content. Gestures, tone, and pacing were all carefully considered to maximize impact. In an age of virtual communication, where body language and vocal variety are often limited, this lesson is more important than ever. By mastering the art of delivery, we can bring our words to life and captivate our audience.

Finally, the Romans remind us that oratory is a moral endeavor. Cicero famously argued that a good speaker must also be a good person, as only someone with integrity can truly inspire trust. This ideal challenges modern speakers to align their words with their values, using their voices to uplift rather than manipulate. The Roman legacy in oratory is a call to greatness, urging us to strive for excellence in both speech and character.

6

Chapter 6: The Silence of the Indus Valley

The Indus Valley Civilization, one of the world's earliest urban societies, remains shrouded in mystery. Despite the absence of deciphered texts, archaeological evidence suggests a sophisticated culture that valued communication and symbolism. Seals and artifacts depict scenes of ritual and governance, hinting at a rich tradition of oral and visual rhetoric. While their words may be lost, their legacy offers valuable lessons for modern speakers.

One of the most striking features of Indus Valley communication is its reliance on visual symbols. The intricate carvings on seals and pottery suggest a language of images, where meaning was conveyed through patterns and motifs. This emphasis on visual rhetoric is particularly relevant today, where infographics, slideshows, and social media dominate communication. By incorporating visual elements into our speeches, we can make our messages more engaging and accessible.

The Indus Valley people also understood the importance of brevity. Their symbols are concise yet powerful, conveying complex ideas with remarkable economy. In an age of information overload, this lesson is invaluable. By distilling our messages to their essence, we can cut through the noise and capture our audience's attention. Sometimes, less truly is more.

Another hallmark of Indus Valley communication is its communal nature. The layout of their cities suggests a culture that valued collaboration and shared spaces. This sense of community is reflected in their artifacts, which often depict group activities and rituals. Modern speakers can draw inspiration from this approach, fostering a sense of connection and participation in their audiences. By creating a dialogue rather than a monologue, we can make our speeches more inclusive and impactful.

Finally, the Indus Valley reminds us that communication is not just about words. Their legacy challenges us to think beyond language, exploring the power of silence, gesture, and symbolism. In a world where words are often overused, this lesson is a powerful reminder of the many ways we can connect with others. The silence of the Indus Valley speaks volumes, urging us to listen not just with our ears but with our hearts.

7

Chapter 7: The Mesoamerican Voice

In the jungles and highlands of Mesoamerica, the Maya and Aztecs developed a rich tradition of oratory that blended speech, ritual, and performance. Their rhetoric was deeply intertwined with their cosmology, reflecting a belief in the power of words to bridge the human and divine realms. From the grand plazas of Tenochtitlán to the sacred temples of Tikal, speech was a vital tool for governance, worship, and storytelling.

One of the most distinctive features of Mesoamerican oratory is its performative nature. Speeches were often accompanied by music, dance, and ritual, creating a multisensory experience for the audience. This holistic approach to communication is particularly relevant today, where audiences crave authenticity and engagement. By incorporating elements of performance into our speeches, we can create a more immersive and memorable experience.

The Mesoamericans also understood the importance of repetition and rhythm. Their speeches often followed a cyclical structure, mirroring the natural cycles of time and the cosmos. This technique not only reinforced key messages but also created a sense of harmony and balance. Modern speakers can draw inspiration from this approach, using rhythm and repetition to make their speeches more compelling and cohesive.

Another hallmark of Mesoamerican rhetoric is its use of metaphor and symbolism. The Popol Vuh, a sacred text of the Maya, is filled with allegories that convey profound truths about life, death, and the human condition. By using metaphor to illustrate abstract ideas, modern speakers can make their messages more relatable and impactful. A well-chosen metaphor can illuminate an idea in a way that plain language cannot.

Finally, the Mesoamericans remind us that oratory is a sacred act. Their speeches were not just about conveying information but about creating a connection with the divine. This sense of reverence is a powerful reminder that words have the power to uplift and inspire. By speaking with sincerity and purpose, we can create a lasting impact that transcends time and space. The Mesoamerican voice is a testament to the enduring power of speech.

8

Chapter 8: The African Echoes

Africa's rich oral traditions are among the oldest and most vibrant in the world. From the griots of West Africa to the storytellers of the Kalahari, speech has long been a cornerstone of African culture. These traditions are not just about entertainment; they are a means of preserving history, imparting wisdom, and fostering community. The African approach to oratory is deeply participatory, emphasizing dialogue and connection over monologue and authority.

One of the most striking features of African rhetoric is its reliance on storytelling. Griots, the revered oral historians of West Africa, use narrative to convey complex ideas and moral lessons. Their stories are not just told but performed, with gestures, music, and audience interaction bringing them to life. Modern speakers can draw inspiration from this approach, using storytelling to make their messages more engaging and relatable. A well-told story can captivate an audience and make abstract concepts tangible.

Another hallmark of African oratory is its emphasis on community. In many African cultures, speech is a communal act, with the audience actively participating in the dialogue. This sense of connection is reflected in the call-and-response format, where the speaker's words are echoed or affirmed by the listeners. By fostering a sense of participation in our speeches, we can create a more inclusive and dynamic experience for our audience.

African rhetoric also highlights the importance of adaptability. Griots and storytellers tailor their messages to the needs and interests of their audience, often improvising to suit the occasion. This flexibility is particularly relevant in today's fast-paced world, where speakers must often adjust their approach on the fly. By being attuned to our audience's reactions, we can ensure that our message resonates and connects.

Finally, the African tradition reminds us that oratory is an act of service. Griots are not just entertainers but custodians of culture and history, using their words to educate and inspire. This sense of purpose is a powerful reminder that the true goal of speech is not to impress but to uplift. By speaking with humility and sincerity, we can create a lasting impact that transcends time and space. The echoes of African oratory are a testament to the enduring power of words.

9

Chapter 9: The Asian Harmony

In the ancient civilizations of Asia, oratory was deeply intertwined with philosophy, spirituality, and governance. From the Confucian scholars of China to the Vedic sages of India, speech was seen as a reflection of inner harmony and moral integrity. The Asian approach to rhetoric emphasizes balance, humility, and the pursuit of truth, offering timeless lessons for modern speakers.

One of the key contributions of Asian rhetoric is its focus on ethical communication. Confucius taught that a good speaker must first be a good person, as only someone with integrity can inspire trust. This principle challenges modern speakers to align their words with their values, using their voices to uplift rather than manipulate. By speaking with sincerity and humility, we can build a genuine connection with our audience.

Another hallmark of Asian oratory is its use of metaphor and allegory. The Tao Te Ching, for instance, uses simple yet profound imagery to convey complex ideas about life and the universe. This reliance on symbolism is particularly relevant today, where audiences are often overwhelmed by information. By using metaphor to illustrate abstract concepts, we can make our messages more accessible and memorable.

Asian rhetoric also emphasizes the importance of listening. In many Asian traditions, speech is seen as a two-way process, where the speaker must also be a attentive listener. This principle is reflected in the concept of "wu wei" in Taoism, or effortless action, which encourages us to speak only when necessary and to let our words flow naturally. By cultivating the art of listening, we can create a more meaningful and authentic dialogue with our audience.

Finally, the Asian tradition reminds us that oratory is an act of harmony. Whether in the courtly debates of ancient China or the spiritual discourses of India, speech was seen as a means of creating balance and order. This sense of harmony is a powerful reminder that the true purpose of oratory is not to dominate but to connect. By speaking with clarity, compassion, and respect, we can create a lasting impact that transcends time and space. The harmony of Asian oratory is a testament to the enduring power of words.

10

Chapter 10: The Native American Spirit

The Native American tradition of oratory is deeply rooted in a reverence for nature, community, and the interconnectedness of all life. From the councils of the Iroquois to the ceremonies of the Lakota, speech was a vital tool for governance, healing, and storytelling. The Native American approach to rhetoric emphasizes authenticity, respect, and the power of the spoken word to create change.

One of the most distinctive features of Native American oratory is its use of metaphor and imagery. Leaders like Chief Seattle used vivid language to convey profound truths about humanity's relationship with the earth. Their speeches were not just about persuasion but about awakening a deeper understanding of the world. Modern speakers can draw inspiration from this approach, using metaphor to make their messages more evocative and impactful.

Another hallmark of Native American rhetoric is its emphasis on respect. In many Native cultures, speech is seen as a sacred act, requiring careful thought and preparation. Speakers are expected to listen as much as they speak, creating a dialogue rather than a monologue. This principle is particularly relevant today, where divisive rhetoric often dominates public discourse. By speaking with respect and humility, we can foster a more inclusive and constructive dialogue.

Native American oratory also highlights the importance of context.

Speeches were often tailored to specific occasions, whether a council meeting, a healing ceremony, or a seasonal celebration. This attention to context ensured that the message was relevant and meaningful. In an age of global communication, where audiences are more diverse than ever, this lesson is invaluable. By understanding the context in which we speak, we can craft messages that resonate with our listeners and address their needs.

Finally, the Native American tradition reminds us that oratory is an act of healing. Their speeches were not just about conveying information but about restoring balance and harmony. This sense of purpose is a powerful reminder that the true goal of speech is not to dominate but to uplift. By speaking with compassion and sincerity, we can create a lasting impact that transcends time and space. The spirit of Native American oratory is a testament to the enduring power of words.

11

Chapter 11: The Renaissance Revival

The Renaissance marked a rebirth of classical rhetoric, as scholars rediscovered the works of ancient orators and adapted them to contemporary contexts. Figures like Erasmus, Thomas More, and Martin Luther used speech to challenge authority, advocate for social change, and inspire intellectual curiosity. This period reminds us that oratory is not just a tool for maintaining the status quo but a catalyst for progress and innovation.

One of the key contributions of Renaissance rhetoric is its emphasis on humanism. Speakers sought to elevate the human spirit, using their words to inspire creativity, curiosity, and critical thinking. This focus on the individual is particularly relevant today, where audiences crave authenticity and connection. By speaking to the human experience, we can create a more meaningful and impactful dialogue.

Another hallmark of Renaissance oratory is its use of wit and humor. Figures like Erasmus and Shakespeare used clever wordplay and satire to challenge conventions and provoke thought. This approach is particularly effective in modern communication, where humor can break down barriers and make complex ideas more accessible. By incorporating wit into our speeches, we can engage our audience and make our messages more memorable.

Renaissance rhetoric also highlights the importance of adaptability. Speakers like Martin Luther tailored their messages to different audiences, using vernacular language to reach the common people. This principle is crucial in today's globalized world, where speakers must often navigate diverse cultural and linguistic contexts. By adapting our style to the needs of our audience, we can ensure that our message resonates and connects.

Finally, the Renaissance reminds us that oratory is an act of courage. Figures like Thomas More and Galileo used their voices to challenge authority and advocate for truth, often at great personal risk. This sense of purpose is a powerful reminder that the true goal of speech is not to conform but to inspire. By speaking with courage and conviction, we can create a lasting impact that transcends time and space. The revival of Renaissance oratory is a testament to the enduring power of words.

12

Chapter 12: The Modern Symphony

In today's fast-paced, interconnected world, the lessons of ancient rhetoric are more relevant than ever. By synthesizing the wisdom of lost civilizations, modern orators can craft speeches that are both timeless and timely. Whether addressing a small group or a global audience, the principles of clarity, authenticity, and respect remain essential. The "Sounds of the Ancients" are not just echoes of the past but a living legacy, offering guidance and inspiration for anyone seeking to harness the transformative power of words.

One of the key challenges of modern oratory is navigating the noise of the digital age. With so much information competing for our attention, it can be difficult to cut through the clutter. The ancients remind us that the power of speech lies not in volume but in resonance. By speaking with clarity and purpose, we can ensure that our message is heard and remembered.

Another hallmark of modern oratory is its global reach. Thanks to technology, speakers can now address audiences across the world, transcending geographical and cultural boundaries. This presents both opportunities and challenges, as we must learn to adapt our messages to diverse contexts. The ancients offer valuable lessons in this regard, reminding us to speak with respect and humility, and to seek common ground with our listeners.

Modern oratory also highlights the importance of authenticity. In an age of curated personas and filtered realities, audiences crave genuine connection.

The ancients remind us that the most powerful speeches are those that come from the heart. By speaking with sincerity and vulnerability, we can create a deeper and more meaningful connection with our audience.

Finally, the modern symphony of oratory is a call to action. The ancients used their voices to inspire change, challenge injustice, and uplift the human spirit. In a world grappling with complex challenges, from climate change to social inequality, this sense of purpose is more important than ever. By speaking with courage and conviction, we can use our words to create a brighter future for all.

The sounds of the ancients are not lost; they are waiting to be heard. By listening to their echoes, we can transform modern oratory into a force for good. This book is an invitation to embark on that journey, to explore the rich tapestry of ancient rhetoric, and to bring its timeless lessons into our lives. Let us begin with an open mind and a willing heart, ready to learn from those who came before us.

Book Description for *"Sounds of the Ancients: How Rhetoric from Lost Civilizations Can Transform Modern Oratory"*

In a world where words are often drowned in noise, *Sounds of the Ancients* takes readers on a journey through time to rediscover the timeless art of oratory. This book is not just a history lesson; it's a guide to unlocking the power of speech by learning from the greatest orators of lost civilizations. From the poetic hymns of Mesopotamia to the philosophical debates of ancient Greece, from the sacred chants of the Maya to the communal storytelling of African griots, each chapter reveals the secrets of rhetoric that have shaped humanity's greatest moments.

Through vivid storytelling and practical insights, *Sounds of the Ancients* shows how the wisdom of the past can transform the way we communicate today. Whether you're a seasoned speaker or someone who struggles to find their voice, this book offers a treasure trove of techniques and principles to help you connect with your audience, craft compelling messages, and inspire change. You'll learn how to balance logic and emotion, how to use metaphor and storytelling to captivate listeners, and how to speak with authenticity and purpose.

CHAPTER 12: THE MODERN SYMPHONY

But this book is more than just a manual for public speaking. It's a celebration of the human spirit and the enduring power of words. It reminds us that oratory is not just about persuasion; it's about connection, understanding, and the shared pursuit of truth. By listening to the echoes of ancient voices, we can find our own voice and use it to make a difference in the world.

Sounds of the Ancients is an invitation to step into the shoes of history's greatest speakers, to walk the paths they walked, and to carry their legacy forward. It's a call to slow down, to choose our words carefully, and to remember that every speech is an opportunity to leave a lasting impact. Whether you're addressing a boardroom, a classroom, or a global audience, this book will inspire you to speak with clarity, courage, and compassion.

Let the sounds of the ancients guide you. Let their wisdom transform your words. And let your voice become part of the symphony that shapes the future.

www.ingramcontent.com/pod-product-compliance
Lightning Source LLC
LaVergne TN
LVHW020743090526
838202LV00057BA/6215